Music CD included with book purchase.

To receive your recording of author Danice Sweet and her group, Revival, singing her songs which she discusses in this book, fill out this coupon and mail it to the address below.

PLEASE PRINT

Name: _____

Street Address: _____

City, State, Zip Code: _____

MAIL TO:

Pearson Publishing Company
711 N. Carancahua, Suite 119
Corpus Christi, Texas 78475

CONSIDER IT JOY

WRITTEN & ILLUSTRATED

BY

DANICE E. SWEET

2007

PEARSON PUBLISHING COMPANY
CORPUS CHRISTI

Copyright © 2007 by Danice E. Sweet

All rights reserved. No part of this book may be reproduced or transmitted in any form or by any means, electronic or mechanical, including photocopy, recording, or any information and storage and retrieval system, without prior written permission from the publisher, except by a reviewer who may quote brief passages in a review.

Library of Congress Control Number: 2007930116

ISBN-10: 0-9768083-9-0 perfect bind
ISBN-13: 978-0-9768083-9-8 perfect bind
ISBN-10: 0-9768083-7-4 e-book
ISBN-13: 978-0-9768083-7-4 e-book

Unless otherwise indicated all scriptures are taken from *The Holy Bible*, New International Version, Zondervan Publishing House, Grand Rapids, Michigan, c1984.

Cover illustration: Danice E. Sweet
Cover design: Katherine Pearson Jagoe Massey
Book design: Katherine Pearson Jagoe Massey

Graphic coordination of cover by Tamara Teas of Graphics, Etc.

Published by
Pearson Publishing Company
Corpus Christi, Texas

www.PearsonPub.US

Danice Sweet is my favorite female bass singer.

I know her as a dedicated Christian and exceptionally talented singer.

Now I know something more.

Danice is also a gifted writer.

This is a short book of brief, punchy chapters.

But each chapter will bless your life.

God bless you, Danice for adding faith, fun and focus
to our daily walk with God.

Write some more!

> Marvin Phillips
> Minister
>
> Phillipians 1:3
>
> "I thank my God upon every
> remembrance of you."

Marvin Phillips is an internationally known speaker, minister, and author of *Never Lick A Frozen Flagpole* and *Never Lick A Moving Blender.*

Other Books by Danice E. Sweet

Floating Zoo and the Whale Motel, written and illustrated by Danice E. Sweet. Pearson Publishing Company, 2006.

Table of Contents

Acknowledgements	xi
Foreword	xiii
Chapter One: A Little Grillin'	1
Chapter Two: A Sign of Spring	5
Chapter Three: How Busy Are You?	9
Chapter Four: Your Greatest Fan	13
Chapter Five: Rolling Over	19
Chapter Six: The Sin of Ungratefulness	23
Chapter Seven: The Shopping List	27
Chapter Eight: Restore My Soul	31
Chapter Nine: On A Mission	35
Chapter Ten: My Big Feet	39
Chapter Eleven: I Brake For Garage Sales	43
Chapter Twelve: A Ray of Sunshine	47
Chapter Thirteen: It's All In The Cards	51
Chapter Fourteen: Hitting A Milestone	57
Chapter Fifteen: Cold in the Valley	61
Chapter Sixteen: Finding Your Ministry	65

Chapter Seventeen: Song Heard 'Round the World 71

Chapter Eighteen: The Healing Power of Prayer 75

Chapter Nineteen: Consider It Pure Joy 77

Chapter Twenty: Don't Wait 'Til Winter 83

Chapter Twenty-one: My Bible and It's Scars 87

Afterword 91

Bibliography 95

Revival Discography 97

Acknowledgments

The author wishes to thank Chet Sweet, my amazing husband who has seen me through more ups than downs and more hills than valleys.

Thanks to my mom and dad who continue to be living examples of what Christ would do to help people on Earth. They have never hesitated to come running, even when we were broken down on a lonely western Kansas highway, and somehow made us feel like we were blessing them with an opportunity to serve.

Special thanks to my sister, Dayna who has faced more adversity than most people on the planet, and still has faith, peace, hope and love.

Thank you to my best friend, Donja for proofreading for me, and for over thirty years, providing more encouragement, than anyone could ask for.

Thank you to my precious niece, Holly, who has amazing faith, strength & belief in the power of prayer.

My sincere gratitude to Terry Lewis and Craig Hayes for the miles we've traveled sharing the good news in song and the encouragement you've given me through your lives, families and faith. I've seen Jesus in you.

Foreword

This book is a collection of thoughts, stories, spiritual songs and what I've learned from them.

I get goose bumps when I hear incredible four-part harmony, see a blank canvas become a beautiful masterpiece, and when I see how God has changed someone's heart.

I've been blessed to see God work in the lives of so many people and situations that I felt compelled to write them down and share them with you. I pray the words are an encouragement and help further your walk with the Lord.

- D.E.S.

Chapter One: A Little Grillin'

A fellow came up to me a few weeks ago. He had lived across the alley from our home, until he rented the house out to another family. He had a musical background, and occasionally I had heard music coming from his garage-turned-into-a-studio. We knew each other by name and usually spoke when we were taking the trash out at the same time. I was surprised when he said, "I need to tell you something."

I stopped and asked, "Well, what would that be?"

I was very curious and wondering why, after years of living within one hundred feet of each other, there was suddenly something he needed to tell me.

"I've been sharing about you as I give my testimony," he replied with a smile. Instantly, I tried to jog my memory, wondering if I had done something that would be mentioned in a court document. Testimony, is not a word we commonly use, but maybe we should.

I inquired, "Your testimony?"

"Yes!" he insisted.

"You may not even remember this, but many years ago, when we lived across the alley from you, I was working with a ministry that was not making enough to cover its expenses or my family's. One evening, we were standing in the kitchen scouring the cabinets for something to feed our two children.

With no money and no food, I lead the family in a prayer. We prayed specifically for that evening meal, having no idea what we would eat or where it would come from.

While we were praying, there was a knock at the door. As I opened the door, you were standing there with a huge plate of grilled meat: hot dogs, hamburgers and chicken breasts. My mouth dropped open, and I don't even know if I spoke to you, I was so overwhelmed.

You simply smiled and said, "This is going to sound crazy, but we just got a new gas grill, and I've been doing a little grillin.' Well actually, I grilled almost everything I could get my hands on. I don't even have a place to put all this. Would your family like to take these off my hands?"

He finished by telling me that he took the tray of meat into the kitchen, and his wife and children were shocked at how quickly God had answered their prayer. He also replied that there was enough food on that tray, for the rest of the week.

Now I remember the gas grill, and I vaguely remember taking a plate of burgers across the alley, along the fence, and up the stairs, but I didn't know until ten years later that God had used me to feed a hungry family of four that evening. I got goose bumps.

He Calls Me His Child

I'm a tree I can bend
When the storm comes rolling in
I'm strong my roots run deep
But when problems come along
There's just a part of me that forgets all He's done
He never does
He never does
He never gives up on the weary
Never gives up on the weak
And everytime I've fallen down

He lifts me to my feet
In your eyes I'm a hopeless case
That is just because
You may have all but given up
He never does

He forgives and forgets
Puts my sins as far as east
Is from the west
And then hopes for the best
There's just a part of me that doubts that great a love
He never does
He never does

And when I feel like hope is gone
His precious mercy comes along
And though I don't deserve His grace and his love
He calls me his child just because
Just because

He never gives up on the weary
Never gives up on the weak
And everytime I've fallen down
He lifts me to my feet
In your eyes I'm a hopeless case
That is just because
You may have all but given up
He never does

(Recorded on Revival's *If That Isn't Love* c.d.)

Chapter Two: A Sign of Spring

We have two flowerbeds in front of our house that get direct sunlight from noon until night. I have tried to plant everything from Spanish moss to pansies, and the only thing that can make it from June to September is vincas. They are not the most beautiful flowers, but with some Miracle-Gro plant food and regular watering, they look pretty decent. We've had a rainy June this year, and my vincas are about six inches tall.

I never thought of myself as a gardener, but I love watching these flowers grow. Never mind that the pansies that were planted in May in the same flowerbeds died a miserable death while we were recording an album in Florida. I came home to a thick, lush green *grass* bed, where the flowers had been.

Not to be defeated, I pulled out every blade of grass and turned over the soil, and one cool June morning I planted pink, white and purple vincas that were at our local Ace Hardware Store and on the 40% off rack. Now I watch my flowers like I'm the periwinkle guard instead of gardener. I have time and money invested in those flowers, and I'm determined to see them reach their full potential. I wonder if God ever looks at me the same way?

"Consider how the lilies grow. They do not labor or spin. If that is how God clothes the grass of the field, which is here today and gone tomorrow, how much more will He clothe you" (Luke 12:27).

There are days, my actions and answers could put me on the 40% off rack.

A little withered.

A little weary.

Don't feel like I've been tended to properly.

Definitely haven't seen enough sunshine.

Certainly allowed the weeds of life to creep in.

The Gracious Gardener of my life, gently steps in, overlooks the weeds, prunes the leaves that are not growing and refreshes me with just what I need:

The Miracle – Gro of a friend's e-mail message that restores hope.

The chirp of a bird outside my window, signaling spring has arrived.

The sight of a rainbow after a thunderstorm, reminding us of God's promise.

A message from His word that reminds me, I'm not perfect, there is only one who has ever been, and I'm not Him.

Perhaps it's time to take a look at the small things we sometimes forget to thank God for.

Over ten years ago a sister in Christ, Andrea Grossinger, gave me a poem that talked about the walls we build up. It inspired this song.

Stone By Stone

Teach me, Lord to hear Your voice
And to listen when You call
And as You take me stone by stone
There will be no wall at all
This wall I've built stands firm and tall
Protects me from my feelings and my failures great and small
And even though sometimes I hide behind this wall
This fortress makes it hard to hear when my Father calls
When friends you love are hard to find
The world seems to hit you, attacking from all sides
We start to build a wall with stones of fear and pride
The spirit longs to intercede, our cries from inside
So Jesus take this wall from me
Remove each stone that I have placed so carefully
With gentle hands the Great I Am will set me free
Then this wall will crumble down and I'll be released

So teach me, Lord to hear Your voice
And to listen when You call
And as You take me stone by stone
There will be no wall at all

(Recorded on Revival's *Stone by Stone* c.d.)

"For He Himself is our peace, who has made the two one and has destroyed the barrier, the dividing wall of hostility."
Ephesians 2:14

Chapter Three: How Busy Are You?

I was leaving Wal-Mart yesterday, and a lady in our community, whom I recognized but couldn't name, asked in passing, "Having a busy summer?" I simply replied, "Always!"

Now, why is that? As a school teacher, summer is often our down time. A chance to relax, refocus, and recharge. I've been tackling several projects at home, with the ultimate goal that I can reward myself when I'm finished by doing what I love, oil painting.

A Native American once said, "If you work with your hands you are a laborer, if you work with your hands and your mind, you are a craftsman, if you work with your hands, your mind, your heart and soul, you are an artist."

A canvas is waiting for me on the back porch. I haven't decided what it is I'm going to paint yet. I just love the idea of starting. Of course, finishing is the hard part. Spreading that paint on that fresh white material, making something out of nothing, creating something that will last after I'm gone; all those feelings make starting a painting very exciting.

What will it become?

Will someone want what I have made and be willing to buy it?

Will it be displayed somewhere special?

Will it evoke an emotion or give someone peace?

As an artist, there is such a joy in the creating process. I don't mind the middle part either. Working on an area to make it look realistic, trying to recreate something the Lord made, like a sunset that is so beautiful, and even adding a bird or squirrel that wasn't in the original photo I'm using as a guide to paint. I'm especially grateful when my husband or a friend, comes in and says, "Whoa! When did you start that?" Or "That is your best one yet!" That just spurs me on to keep working.

Time goes by, and I realize darkness has fallen, the light has changed, and I've been painting for hours, without a glass of tea or a phone call or a break. It's that finishing part that gets me almost every time.

Perhaps that is why I can relate to Dan Fogelburg's song, "Along the Road:"

> 'On the road your path may wander, pilgrim's faith may fail, absence makes the heart grow fonder, darkness obscures the trail.'

When my faith begins to falter, it's not usually at the beginning or in the middle, it's toward the end. When the journey is almost over, when I'm so close to the goal, when I'm toward the end of the trail. That is when I begin to doubt myself, and the One who made me. My cousin sent me this scripture in an e-mail: Ecclesiastes 10:4 ".... calmness can lay great errors to rest."

I was sitting in a funeral chapel recently and realized how quiet it was and how long it had been since I had just meditated. I mean, really sat somewhere quietly and thought about God's word, his strength, and His love.

I started praying silently, as I waited for the service to begin. I prayed for the widow and the family. I prayed for my friend whose mother was just diagnosed with a brain tumor. I prayed for my husband and the stresses of his new job while finishing classes two nights a week at a college an hour away. As I concluded my prayer and the music for the funeral began, a woman started singing, "Blessed Assurance." I knew what she meant.

"...this is my story, this is my song, praising my Savior all the day long..."

I felt a peace I had not known in three months. I smiled and nodded my head as the minister shared the details of this man's life and sixty-five years of marriage through valleys and hills, successes and failures. That was his story; that was his song. All of us were sitting there paying our respects to someone for a life well lived.

It took that time of calmness, for me to finally sit still, to listen, to breathe and to lay errors to rest.

There was a wonderful movie years ago starring Robert Duvall. It was about a man who had lived a hard life and needed a second chance. There was a woman similar to the one described in Proverbs 31 who continued to work, serve, and imitate Christ until his heart changed. I loved the title of it, "Tender Mercies". That and my mother inspired this song.

Tender Mercies

His tender mercies rest upon me
Though I'll never be worthy of it all
He has shown His grace
And someday I'll see His face
And His tender mercies will upon me fall
Each day I'll strive a little harder
Wanting to be more like Him
Wanting to do more than barely make it
Certain that when my life ends

His tender mercies rest upon me
Though I'll never be worthy of it all
He has shown His grace
And someday I'll see His face
And his tender mercies will upon me fall
Having tried and having fallen
He picks me up without complaint
Knowing I won't reach perfection
'Til I see those pearly gates
I know, I know I don't deserve what I've been given
So I need to share with you
His tender mercies rest upon me
Though I'll never be worthy of it all
He has shown His grace
And someday I'll see His face
And His tender mercies will upon me fall

(Recorded on Revival's *Knockin' At Your Door* c.d.)

Chapter Four: Your Greatest Fan

She was about five foot two inches tall, but you could spot her in a sea of over two thousand bluegrass festival fans sitting in their lawn chairs waiting for the next group. She always had on one of our group's t-shirts and a matching hat with our group name, Revival. But the one way you could spot her every time was that huge smile, grinning from ear to ear, leaning next to a complete stranger, saying, "That's her: the redhead up there; she's my daughter- in- law."

If we were singing within a fifty mile radius of home, she was there, front row center; our greatest fan. I had always heard about mothers-in-law. The jokes, the sit-coms, the stories many people told. But those never applied to me. My mother-in-law was the most giving woman I have ever known. You could not walk out of her house empty handed. It was impossible.

She was an Avon lady, and would purchase extra lotions and perfumes to keep gifts and supplies on hand for customers. If you mentioned a shower gel or moisture therapy hand cream you enjoyed, out came this huge paper sack, and she would begin to fill it. Everything from homemade salsa, or my husband's favorite homemade chicken and noodles, or scalloped potatoes, along with any Avon product she knew you loved, would fill up that sack.

You could try to pay her for the Avon, you could argue, you could even leave money in a subtle spot, but you could not get out the door without an armload. That was her way. I'd receive cards, letters and little notes just thanking me for loving her son, for stopping by when I was in town, or in gratitude for calling about a recipe.

She had lived a life filled with heartache and trials, often working three jobs at a time to support four kids on her own. When my husband became a Christian, he started studying with his mother. It wasn't long before he had the privilege of baptizing her into Christ.

Several years later, we received the call from the hospital. My husband called me from work and was heading there as fast as he could. He made it in time to see her take her last breath. Days later, the Lord put this song on my heart, and we sing it often in concert. It is rare for me to get through it without tears.

Hurry Home

I was playing tag outside
With some kids down the street
Didn't notice it was getting dark
Heard her call for me

Hurry home, I've been waiting here for you
Hurry home, there's so much we've got to do
The light is on, the table's set
I've been worried half to death
Waiting here for you
So hurry home

Years later I went off to school
I couldn't wait to leave
Missing home when I called her up
Here's what she said to me

Hurry home, I've been waiting here for you
Hurry home, there's so much we've got to do
The light is on, the table's set
I've been worried half to death
Waiting here for you
So hurry home

Got the call it was almost noon
They said you better run
Her body had just given out
She asked to see her son
As I stood there silently
Stroked her hair and felt her leave
Thought I could hear my momma plead

Hurry home, I've been waiting here for you
Hurry home, there's so much we've got to do
The light is on, the table's set

Don't be worried 'bout my death
I'll be waiting here
So hurry home

The light is on, the table's set
Don't be worried about my death
I'll be waiting here
When you get home

(Recorded on Revival's *Best of Revival* cd.)

As that song has been sung, I've seen audiences of men and women and even children brought to tears.

I picture God waiting for us in Heaven.

The light is on. The table is set, and every trial we go through, is another opportunity for Him to let us know we are not alone. There is someone cheering for us, knowing we may slip and fall, but confident we will get up again. He is your greatest fan.

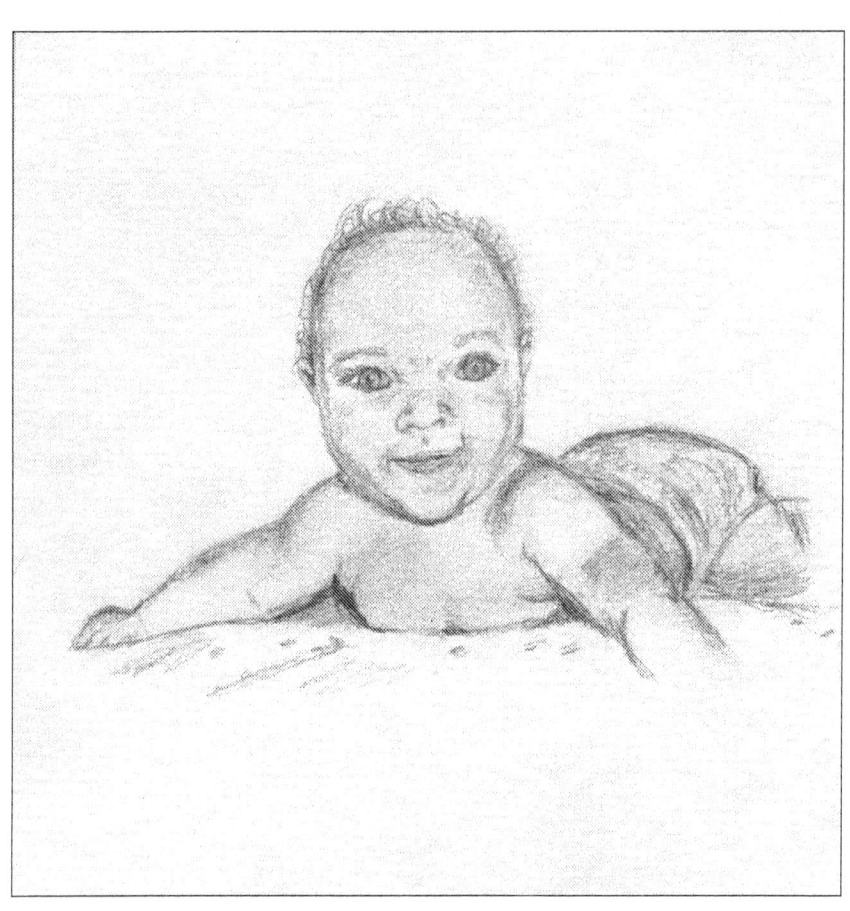

Chapter Five: Rolling Over

My great nephew is on his way to crawling. He is rolling over and always acts surprised when, after getting the momentum going, he ends up on his stomach. He gets excited, then scared and then starts to cry. However, when you put him on his back, the whole process starts again.

Not unlike how we might look to God, Our Father.

I'm often on my way, I get excited about a project, then scared and yes, sometimes start to cry, and I'm often surprised where I end up.

Like an infant, we don't see the outcome clearly.

Whether it's an electrical outlet, or a bumblebee, or rolling over, it may look exciting, but when we get there, it may be dangerous.

How many Christians have encountered the same problem in their lives? It looks so good, so enticing, but what we don't know could change our lives forever.

Our Christian music group was on the road several years ago to Athens, Texas. As the highway curved, we noticed a trailer that looked amazingly like our own, passing us on the right, rolling over and coming to a stop. When the knowledge finally sank in that it was indeed our trailer and all of our sound equipment and tapes and compact discs are at a ninety degree angle off a Texas highway, and we are three hours away from praising God in song, it is gut wrenching. While getting on the cellular phone and contacting the people at the church, a man pulled up in a white commercial Texas Highway Department truck. I honestly thought he was sent by someone we called. In a manner of speaking, he was.

He happened to be driving home from work. He happened to have a winch on the truck that could pull the trailer upright again, and he happened to have the same trailer hitch on his truck that we did on our van. He also lived only fifteen minutes from where we were going and also could take the time to bring our trailer to the church so we could get the equipment set up in time for the concert that evening.

As this Good Samaritan was heading down the highway with our trailer filled with equipment, my husband, Chet, who is also our soundman, questioned,

"How did you get him here so fast?"

I responded, "I didn't get him here at all, he just pulled up to help."

Chet started speeding up to catch up with the truck. "You mean all of our sound equipment is hooked to the truck of someone we don't even know?"

I simply said, "The Lord provided."

"Let's hope the Lord doesn't provide him with all of our equipment," Chet said cautiously.

We made it safely, so did our equipment, and the man would not take any money for all the help he gave us.

We still pass that curve when we go back to Athens, Texas. We all turn around and check the back window to make sure the trailer is still attached.

Tomorrow I go in for a breast biopsy. Two lumps are abnormal, and I'm scared. I know that's natural. I also know what God has brought me through. Regardless of the result, I know he holds the future, the present and my past.

He is the same yesterday, today and forever.

Zephaniah 3:17

The Lord God is with you,
The mighty one will save you
He will rejoice over you.
You'll rest in His love and He will sing and be joyful about you.
Zephaniah 3:17.

(Recorded on Revival's *Show Me The Cross* c.d.)

Chapter Six: The Sin of Ungratefulness

Beside my bed, I keep a note pad for messages to clear my head before I go to sleep. Tonight it reads,

Go to the bank.
Mail bills.
Visit Grandma.
   (Don't forget to swing by McDonalds and get a bag of those
   Apple Dippers she likes.)
Study and prepare for tomorrow's Vacation Bible School class.
Read the next chapter in Max Lucado's, It's Not About Me.

I'm not normally a list person. I grew up in a house with lists. My mother's middle name is "Organization." She honestly has everything in the medicine cabinet in alphabetical order: aspirin, backaches, cough syrup, all the way to zinc oxide cream.

The chores were posted on the fridge, and everyday there was a chore to dread. Mom was a schoolteacher and hated the word "BORED!" If during the summer, while she was taking classes, we mentioned how bored we were, my sister and I had the privilege of dusting every base board in our two-story house. You know what I'm talking about…the wooden trim at the bottom of the walls of old houses? Well, this house had seven gables, and the upstairs functioned as a separate apartment before my folks bought it. Needless to say, we learned very quickly to take that word out of our vocabulary. We might say something like, " we longed for something else to fill our summer hours," but we never said the word, "bored" again.

We had bicycles to ride, friends to see, art classes to take, swimming lessons to go to, but give us one hour at home, and we became listless. That's of course, when my sister and I would start fussing and fighting.

The dividing of the chores was a constant source of discussion. Even though the chart stated which one we had to do, we were always bargaining for the easiest route to follow. Taking out the trash didn't take long, but dishes were the worst. We always fussed about the dishes. If I wanted to wash, she wanted to wash. If I wanted to dry, she wanted to dry. I always seemed to get the "sticky day dishes." If my sister had to wash on fish stick night, then I had to wash on spaghetti night. It just never seemed fair.

It took some time for me to realize how ungrateful I was. It actually took traveling on a missionary trip to Ukraine, for me to understand how I have been committing the sin of ungratefulness.

I should have been grateful that we even had a fish stick night. Instead, I complained that we had to eat my mother's sugar free pumpkin cookies that she was experimenting with as a Weight Watcher lecturer, rather than the Twinkies my friend had at her house.

I didn't comprehend how blessed we were to live in a house, have a choice of sneakers to wear, and to sleep in our own beds.

The issue of gratitude has everything to do with loving and giving. Many years ago, my husband worked as a sound man for a Christian music group. He was working over 200 hours a week, with very little sleep for even less pay. I was so concerned about his health, I finally asked, "How can you do this, they don't even appreciate you?" He replied, "I'm not doing this for the company, I'm doing this for the Lord."

"Be joyful always, pray continually, give thanks in all circumstance for this is God's will for you in Christ Jesus."
(I Thessalonians 5:16 --18)

Sums it up pretty well, doesn't it? Not always easy though. I've spent the last several years trying to be more grateful. Christian parents, a thoughtful sister, a loving husband, a home with heat during winter and air conditioning in the summer, electricity at the flip of a switch, and water we can drink right from the faucet. These are a few of the many reasons I praise God.

While hiking through Golden, Colorado, I became breathless, forgetting what the high altitude can do to you. I sat down on a rock and looked at the orange and pink sun beginning to rise over the mountaintops and wrote this down.

Reasons I Praise You

The breathtaking beauty of Your mountains
Your waving fields of golden grain
The ocean foaming at my feet
The fragrance of rain smells so sweet
These are a few reasons I praise You

I praise You Lord, for times I feel like this
I worship You with all I am,
Remind me please
That moments like these only come
When we start to worship You

The friends and the loved ones we hold dearly
The family in Christ we've come to know
The chance we have to praise Your name
And tell the world why Jesus came
These are a few reasons I praise You

Days won't always be this bright
Skies not always clear,
But in life's uncertainties
We can feel You near

I praise You Lord, for times I feel like this
I worship You with all I am, Remind me please
That moments like these only come
When we start to worship You

(Recorded on Revival's *Song Heard 'Round The World* c.d.)

Chapter Seven: The Shopping List

I sat in on a discussion with a group of ladies one Sunday morning, as they were trying to decide on a project to reach out to the community. As I followed the suggestions and conversations, each idea was shot down as quickly as it was brought up. I could see that it was not going to be easy to come up with a project the majority would support.

Suddenly a woman jumped to her feet and said, "What we need is something that makes the church look good. We must improve our reputation in this area!"

Her statement was met with verbal agreement from many in the room. I tilted my head and began to think, "Are *WE* not '*THE CHURCH?*'" Has she not actually stated that we need to make ourselves *look good?*

Now, I know I may be oversimplifying, but the whole thing rubbed me the wrong way. We're not here to make ourselves look good, no matter what magazine advertisers say or what television depicts. *WE are here to GLORIFY GOD!*

A missionary once told me, that we are the only creatures that don't naturally praise God:

> The flowers glorify him by growing and reaching for the sun.
> The birds compliment him by chirping.
> Even the crickets rub their legs together to create nature's symphony.

But humans, well, we have to be reminded.

Remember your creator in the days of your youth. If anyone is happy, he should sing songs of praise...

David in Psalm 89:5 says,
"The heavens praise Your wonders, O Lord."

Why doesn't it come more naturally for us? I must admit that I have gotten in the habit of forgetting to praise Him when I pray. I just start right in with my wants and desires and hopes and dreams and then realize it must sound like a shopping list to God:

Protect me as I travel.
Help Dad with his blood pressure.
Give Mom peace about the grandkids.
Help my friend find a Christian mate.
And somewhere in there, uh, thank you for the roof over my head, and food in the fridge, and a car that runs.
In Jesus name, Amen.

Years ago I heard a group in Tennessee sing a song that I've never forgotten. It's a spoof on the way so many of us pray and I think it makes a great point:

The cattle on a thousand hills, they all belong to You,
I don't need any cows right now, but something else will do,
Give me this, give me that
Bless me Lord I pray
Grant me what I think I need
To make it through the day.
Keep me healthy
Make me wealthy
Give me what I missed
On my never ending shopping list,
My, my, my never-ending shopping list.

Sound familiar? I know my prayers do at times. They sound more like a trip to Wal-Mart than a petition to the Father. I spend far too much time asking for things rather than praising the Almighty.

I think God must feel neglected when that is all I see Him as: someone to whom I can run when things get rough, someone who is never too busy to hear me whine, someone who knows when I'm ready to give in and give up on everything and everyone. He doesn't want to simply be my counselor, or adviser, much less my cashier at life's check-out counter, but my Lord.

He wants to be the first one I think of when I wake up in the morning, the reason I do a good deed or think of others first, the hope that fills my heart when the world turns against me, the last one I think of before I go to sleep. He wants my life to be a worship service to Him.

I wrote this song after hearing a discussion on the way we should worship God. Worship should not be an hour each week at a building or five acts that must be completed before calling it "full-fledged worship." Worship must be a life long process: a way to perceive how we affect others in view of God's mercy toward us. It should be a grateful response to all that God has done and will do.

Worship with Your Life

Sing a song, say a prayer
Have we forgotten what we're doing here
Does anybody really even care
Is this what worship is?
Quiet time on your knees
Begging to the Father hear my plea
Forgive my sinful tendencies
Is this what worship is?
Worship with your life,
Keep it shining bright,
So they can see the love inside
Worship with your life.
Go to church, you do your best
Have you even thought about the rest
I think it's time for us to confess,
Is this what worship is?
We take the bread and the vine
Does the Savior even cross your mind?
Are you merely putting in your time,
Is this what worship is
Do we focus on appearances
Acting like we're so devout
Or are we looking on the inside,
That's what loves about
Worship with your life,
Keep it shining bright,
So they can see the love inside
Worship with your life.

(Recorded on Revival's *Best of Revival* c.d.)

Chapter Eight: Restore My Soul

I woke up around three in the morning; it was cold, and our bedroom had no heat. We had wall heaters in the living room and kitchen, but we depend on a portable heater for the bedroom that is often unproductive. Winter had arrived, and my lungs could not handle the cold air. I was sore from coughing, and I was praying pneumonia would not set in for the third time.

I finally got up and made myself some orange spice tea, warmed it for about forty seconds, and sat at my desk with my *Women's Devotional Bible*. I just started turning the pages, hoping something would catch my eye, or that I would find a devotional I had not yet read.

There on page 1044, in the middle of Matthew 14, was a little segment called "Weekending." The Zondervan editors put in poems, and scriptures and proverbs for your own Bible study.

The subtitles grabbed my attention:
    Recharge.
    Restore.
    Revive.
That sounded like the prescription I needed.

I wanted the Lord to recharge my heart and give me strength again so I could make it to teach school the next day. I wanted Him to restore my lungs, so the cold air would not make me cough so hard I might break a rib. I needed him to revive my spirit so I could make it through another day without letting the worries of my health, unpaid bills, or anything else zap my joy.

Within five minutes, the Lord put this next song, words and music together on my heart.

Last month while in Texas, a dear sister came to me and told me she spoke at a Women's Lectureship in Abilene, Texas and the song was the catalyst for her lesson. I'm so grateful it touched her heart, and I've included it here in hopes it might speak to you.

Restore My Soul

Restore my soul
Revive my spirit
Recharge my heart
So I can hear it when You call
Restore my soul
Revive my spirit
Hear this simple childlike prayer,
Restore my soul
Restore my soul
Revive my spirit,
Lord recharge my heart oh God
Restore my soul

(Recorded by Revival on *Never Grow Old* c.d.)

Chapter Nine: On a Mission

I have had the incredible opportunity to go on two missionary trips to Ukraine. Our first trip involved traveling to Donetsk and helping a small church that had been started there.

While I was teaching a children's Bible class in a very small basement of an apartment building, the children started getting too loud. There was only a wooden and glass door that separated us from the other room in the basement where the adults were having a Bible Study. I asked my interpreter, Lyuba, to thank the children for working quietly. She looked at me very puzzled and responded, "But they are not working quietly." I asked her once again, please tell them, "Thank you for working quietly."

Teaching elementary school children in Kansas for over fifteen years, I had been taught early on about positive reinforcement. If you encourage and expect the behavior that you want, you are more likely to receive it.

Lyuba finally granted my request, and in Russian announced, "Thank you for working quietly. Every child stopped talking, looked up at Lyuba, then looked at me and began working quietly on their three dimensional Noah's Ark designs.

Lyuba leaned over and whispered, "Does this work in America?" I smiled and replied, "Most of the time."

Some things do not translate well.

Some things do.

On this same journey, we took a fourteen-hour train ride from Kiev, Ukraine to Donetsk. There were fields of sunflowers and small communities and farms, but one scene caught my eye. As the sun was sinking, I saw two women up on a hill sitting on a small bench. Both were wearing head scarves, and I saw them nod and talk to one another like old friends do.

I couldn't help but think about their lives and wonder how many sunsets they had watched together and how many times had they shared their trials and concerns. I contemplated whether they had children or husbands, or whether they had gardens or worked in factories. It dawned on me, how similar we were. Though eight thousand miles from my home, I realized that we all long for peace and happiness and companionship.

I Must Share Jesus

I must share Jesus to all who will listen
To all who are hungry and searching for His word
I must share Jesus to all who are thirsting
'Til His life giving water and healing power
Cover the Earth
We stare at the same moon
We awake to the same sun
We all search for something
That this world just cannot give
But His love knows no language
No nation no color
It has no fences, walls or borders
To keep it in
He gave us His life's blood
He gave us His spirit
He gave us the one thing
To take away our sin
Still His blood knows no language
No nation, no color
It has no fences walls or borders
To keep it in

(Inspired on a train on our first mission trip to Ukraine and recorded on Revival's *Song Heard 'Round The World* c.d.)

Chapter Ten: My Big Feet

I had a scary experience yesterday. I was waiting to pull out into traffic, and suddenly my vehicle lurched forward coming inches away from an oncoming car. I put the Suburban in reverse as quickly as possible, and it happened again. I finally looked down at my foot on the gas pedal and realized my leather sandals were hitting both the gas and the break simultaneously.

It takes fairly large feet to accomplish this. An advantage to having big feet is the size you need is often the last one remaining at a shoe sale. Not a huge demand for women's tens or elevens. However, sometimes it is difficult to get down a flight of stairs if the carpenter was limited on space and had to make them very short. You almost have to place your feet at an angle to get up or down the stairs. I've even been a little self-conscious at times since I happen to wear the same size shoe as my dad.

I received an interesting request by way of a phone call a while back. A preacher friend called and asked, "What size shoes do you wear?"

I was intrigued by the question and replied, "Ten and a half or eleven, depending on the shoe."

"I think that will work," came his reply.

"What are you talking about?" I responded.

He went on to explain that an older woman had called the church and had circulation problems with her feet. She could not afford any shoes for winter and could not find her size at any charity stores in the area. She needed some that had already been broken in so they would not hurt her feet. He had been talking to my parents and mentioned the call, and of course without hesitation, my mother chimed in, "Danice has big feet and lots of shoes; give her a call!"

I gathered up sneakers and loafers and a pair of fluffy house shoes that I thought might work and took them by this woman's home. You would have thought she had won the lottery.

What was taking up space in my closet was now an answer to a needy woman's prayer. I never thought big feet would ever give me a chance to serve the Lord in some way. Consequently, whenever I purchase a new pair of shoes, in order to make a place for them in my closet, I try to pick out a pair that I can take to the woman who called. I wish I could say I was more giving and thoughtful and automatically gave when I knew there was a need, but it took someone who put someone else's needs first, for me to kick in.....pardon the pun.

I come from an emotional family. Yes, we're criers. Movies, special moments, phone calls, departures, even commercials. It's true. We can weep with the best of them. If I see my mama crying, I'm already teary-eyed. My husband has come to accept it, after twenty years. There is no telling what started it, or caused it, but it seems like I go through phases where I cry on a daily basis. Not just sad cries. Sometimes happy, even ecstatic crying. Having been diagnosed with diabetes, occasionally I'll start crying because of low blood sugar. It's so frustrating to be unable to express that I need some juice, or something to bring my blood sugar back up.

Being emotional and a crier, it's sometimes hard to tell what the problem is, even for me. We finally worked out a system. If I can't speak or answer yes or no, then it's blood sugar. My close friends and family know to find something quickly before I pass out. Sometimes my hands or jaw will start shaking, and that's a sure sign.

I remember driving away the first time to a four year college. I was only going to be two hours from home, but I knew it was a new stage in my life. Since then I've seen my share of goodbyes and sung at more than my share of funerals. I don't think it is ever easy to say goodbye, unless you know that loved one was hurting. God put this song on my heart, and I can't help but write this and think of all the loved ones waiting for us to get home.

Never Say Goodbye

Never say goodbye
Never say goodbye
When the journey's over
We won't have to cry cause we'll never say goodbye
Down here below the trials come and they beat me down everyday but we know that a day will come when the Savior will take us away

I've got friends and they don't know that Jesus is the way
It's up to me to make it known
That there will come a day

Don't you want to come with me a sweet reunion there will be
Every eye will all be dry
Will never say goodbye
Come along and join with me
Will praise the Lord eternal
Will shout and sing with Him on high we'll never say goodbye

(Recorded on the *Best of Revival* c.d.)

Chapter Eleven: I Brake for Garage Sales

"Honesty is the best policy."

How often have we heard that?

So often that I thought it was Biblical. It actually comes from Richard Whately, who was once an Archbishop of Dublin.

Growing up in Kansas, one of our Saturday morning rituals was going to the yard sales listed in the newspaper. I had the job of coordinating the best route with the least back tracking. We would always drive very slowly passed the ones that looked 'questionable,' looking to see if the items were neatly stacked or checking to see if anything caught our eye.

Some were vetoed if we only saw clothes, or others with crafts would entice us to pull over and get out and rummage through the goodies.

My favorite memory of a garage sale was once when we went to a house in the country. Those in the country were always a gamble because of the extra driving and too few directions. At this particular sale, we were looking around at the sale items and suddenly a woman asked my mom, "Do you have a fat fanny?"

I could tell mom was trying to ignore the question, hoping it was pointed in someone else's direction.

"DO YOU HAVE A FAT FANNY?" came the question again, only louder.

Mom could ignore it no longer, "Excuse me?" she replied while turning around to find a former school cafeteria employee who was pointing to one of those wooden yard ornaments that resemble someone bending over to do gardening. Mom started laughing as the red color left her cheeks from embarrassment, and then she responded, "Well, I may have one, but I certainly don't need another."

Honesty may be the best policy, but it is often painful as well.

While I was traveling the country with a Christian music group, a well-dressed woman came back to the table where we were selling tapes and c.d.'s after the concert.

"Honey", she said, "I would love to help you with your hair color."

Now I was always proud to be a redhead. My mom's redheaded, several of my aunts are redheaded, my grandfather on my dad's side was redheaded, and only two percent of the nation is redheaded. Some people actually pay to have hair the color of mine, and I couldn't help but be a little offended and a little surprised at the insinuation that my hair color needed help. "Thank you, but it's natural and I'm quite happy with it."

She shrugged and began to leave but before she left she responded, "Well, I could definitely do something about your make-up!"

I was shocked. Looking back, I guess I should have been grateful she was offering her services which I'm sure she considered one of her talents. The fellows I sang with couldn't help but overhear the conversation and the joke for the week was: "Anyone need help? I'd love to help you with your hair color."

Now, I've never thought of myself as thin-skinned. Fair skinned, definitely. Freckled, you bet. But thin-skinned?

Well, that woman's comments have stuck with me for over sixteen years. I couldn't tell you one positive comment that was received after that evening's concert, but I will never forget the hair and make-up one.

How quickly do we respond to a positive word of encouragement?

I began drawing pictures when I was a kid. I won my first art contest when I was eight years old. *The Emporia Gazette* had a contest and the winner received ten dollars and their picture went on the front page of the newspaper. I won and have been drawing ever since. I was rewarded for that behavior and continue to receive a paycheck as an art teacher.

Unfortunately, far too many times we focus on the negative:

> A member of the high school football team, making fun of a self-conscious teenager.

> A boss who repeatedly states, "How many times do I have to show you how it's done?"

> A parent whom you never could please, no matter how hard you tried.

The Hebrew writer says, "Encourage one another all the more as you see the day approaching."

I can't begin to count the number of days I made it through because of someone's encouragement. Someone took the time to tell me they were praying for me or my family or a situation.

The following song has been dedicated to many people over the years. But it was inspired by a young man who sang with us. He found himself without a place to live, without a job and desperate. He lived with us for several months and during one of our late night conversations, I tried to give him hope. This is what the Lord put on my heart:

Praying for You

Tonight you feel like the world's coming in on you
No one can understand what you're going through
But I want you to know that wherever you are
Some where in the world
I'm praying for you
I'm praying that He'll lead you
Right where you need to be
I'm praying He'll guide you through this storm
And while I'm on my knees I'll be lifting you in prayer
I hope wherever you are
You're praying for me

I wish I could be right there to comfort you now
Lord knows I would if I could somehow
So I sing this song for you and where ever you go
You will always know
I'm praying for you

And if my time should come
Before I've time to show
What you've meant to me on Earth
I still want you to know
Even though I can't be seen
There's something I can do
With the Lord in Heaven
We're praying for you
I know where ever I am
I'll be praying for you

(Recorded on Revival's *Knockin' At Your Door* c.d.)

Chapter Twelve: A Ray of Sunshine

I headed out early one Sunday morning to worship with my friend and her family who lived about an hour away. It was cool and cloudy, and the sky was completely gray. Suddenly a ray of sunshine burst onto the windshield from out of nowhere. Not another ray of sunlight in the sky except what was shining on my face. I thanked the Lord for the ray of light, and a song by country singer Billy Dean came on the radio entitled, "If There Hadn't Been You."

I started thinking. If there hadn't been a God in Heaven who decided to send His son to Earth to redeem us, there would be no sight, no sound, no hope. Every sky would be gray. Everything we attempted to do would be of little or no value.

The Lord put this song on my heart that Sunday morning, and as soon as I arrived at the church building, I grabbed a sheet of paper and started writing this song.

If There Were No You

If there were no You my songs would be in vain
If there were no You my skies would all be gray
No hope of life could be found
There would be no sight no sound
There would be no Love,
If there were no You

They questioned whether Jesus was God's son
They even asked Him long ago
With all that He had done
Who gave You authority,
My father who has sent Me
He gave His life and proved He was the One

I've read where the stone was rolled away
The tomb was sealed and secured
Then on the third day
He is risen as He said,
He's alive no longer dead
Since He lives we rejoice and say

If there were no You my songs would be in vain
If there were no You my skies would all be gray
No hope of life could be found
There would be no sight no sound
There would be no Love,
If there were no You

For without You life would have no meaning and without You
I'd have never known amazing grace was for a wretch like me
If there were no You, how could Heaven be my home

(Recorded on Revival's *Show Me The Cross* c.d.)

"And God will generously provide all you need. Then you will always have everything you need and plenty left over to share with others." 2 Corinthians 9:8 (MSG)

Chapter Thirteen: It's All In The Cards

I was playing pinochle with a ladies group last night. We've been playing for twenty years. (Yes, I started very young)

Anyway, I looked around the room and listened to the conversations of women with varying ages of 35 to 70 years old. The group started as an opportunity for ladies from church to gather for fellowship. As fate would have it, the church congregation split nine years ago, but the card playing ladies still get together the second Tuesday of each month as if nothing ever happened.

There are traditions, like a high and low prize for high score and low score, and people who try to win both. If you are having a bad night, as in bad cards, you say, "Well, I'm trying for low."

We always draw cards at random from 1-12 which determines where you start at one of the three card tables, but more importantly, determines who starts the food line. Number one of course is first, etc.

There is a hostess each month who brings the main dish and the prizes, and last night the hostess did not bring a main dish or prizes, and the group was very distraught. Should someone pull the person aside and explain to her that these are her duties as hostess, or should she be asked to host another month since she "didn't fulfill her duties"? One lady always brings soda pop, one always brings ice, one always brings bar code food.

What is bar code food, you ask? Well, that's my mom's forte'. With a doctor's degree, she prefers to run by the grocery store and grab a $9.99 veggie tray to anything home cooked. Home-cooked, a term in our household that meant burnt, bad, why don't we have a dog who we could give this to instead of our finicky cat?

When we saw a sign on a restaurant that said, "Just like Mom Made", we not only kept on driving, we sped up! It's true.

So occasionally I really bake something and shock the whole bunch. I even had someone ask for one of my recipes; that was a first!

Well, back to ladies pinochle. The unspoken criteria for member selection, once was: goes to church, comes on time, always brings her share, plays by the rules. As the group has aged, some have started slipping. We don't call them cheaters, we just say, "she's not up to par."

Some try to out do the others, like serving Cornish hens on Christmas china, while others grill burgers and use paper plates. Regardless, no one curses or smokes, and you must talk trash! No, we don't discuss styrofoam cups or the local landfill. You know, we talk up how we had that last hand won had it not been for so-and-so distracting us with talk of her new ring, or grandbaby or the newest recipe.

What I love about this group of ladies is unity. When someone is hurting or experiences a tragedy, we all come together. Whether it is purchasing flowers during an illness, or taking meals to a home, I know there are eleven other ladies praying for me and who will be there for me, no matter what.

"The temperature of the spiritual life of the church is the index of her power to heal."

These words by Evelyn Frost remind me of the strength and power of women when they pray. I look forward to going to these gatherings, and it takes precedence over things I don't want to go to, like literacy council meetings, Home Interior parties, or Pampered Chef invitations. All of those things are good. I just don't like sitting in uncomfortable chairs with people I don't know, buying things I don't need. A simple reply like, "I have a previous commitment," is all it takes. This pinochle game is very convenient when you want it to be. We never bring children, grandchildren, nieces, etc., but they can stop by to visit or nibble on the snacks.

A strange twist has occurred in the last year. As some of the ladies have moved away or poor vision due to cataracts has stopped their card playing, we've had to resort to male substitutes, usually spouses.

Sounds strange when I write it out, but that is the norm of this group. I miss it being just women. It changes some of our conversations. Not because men are not welcome, (most are also in a monthly gourmet couples pinochle group as well), but the men have started winning high prize every time they fill in. What are they going to do with hand-stitched tea towels, knitted doilies, potpourri? Give them to their wives?

Then we all go home and our husbands ask, "Who was high woman?" and we hang our heads and reply, "Melvin, again!"

This song poured out of my heart as quickly as I could write it down. It was at a time when our local church was experiencing a split that divided families and broke hearts.

Humbly

Humbly
I've a request to make
If I could dear Lord
It makes me ache to see the way we quarrel
We've got so much to do
We've got to tell the world about You
And if You could only see us through tomorrow

We've got brothers fighting brothers
And sisters who don't even talk,
I know it's not the way you planned our walk

Together here,
We've got to help each other or
We're never going to make it there I'm begging you please,
On my knees

Humbly
We're fighting over little things
It's doing nobody good
Tell me why can't we stop judging one another
It comes down to love
And being more like You
So that we can all be one and love each other
Jesus wept over Jerusalem
And I'm crying out today,
I don't know what else I can do but pray
While we fight amongst ourselves
The whole world goes by
And most of them don't know the name of Jesus
It's got to start with You
It's got to start with me
I'm begging you please
Humbly

(Recorded on Revival's *Whatcha Gonna Do About It* c.d.)

This song came to me at a very difficult time in my life. It arrived in my heart and mind within minutes of getting in our van as we were leaving a church camp where we had given a concert.

I thought of so many churches that were dividing over issues that seemed so unimportant. The Book of Romans states, "have nothing to do with foolish controversies," and yet you see them in cities and churches and families all over the world.

I know that is not what God wants to see when He looks down on his children. We had sisters in our home congregation at that time that sat on opposite sides of the building and did not speak to each other. Years go by and you realize how much you've lost. Relationships, memories, hopes, and you can't even remember why an argument even started.

Chapter Fourteen: Hitting a Milestone

You know you are getting older when:
    Your pharmacist says, "Weren't you my babysitter?"

You know you are getting older when:
    Policeman look like they should still be in the Boy Scouts.

You know you are getting older when:
    Your first car can qualify for an antique tag license.

You know you are getting older when:
    You visit a church and the usher shows you to the "over forty" class.

You know you are getting older when:
    You now have the children of past students you once had in class.

You know you are getting older when:
    You hear your favorite song in an elevator.

You know you are getting older when:
    You remember when you didn't know what a microwave was. In fact, your mom said, "Don't stand too close to that thing, they still don't know if it is dangerous."

I recently hit a milestone.

A friend said, it is the decade when you have officially "arrived." I won't share with you which decade that is. However, it is a strange feeling. There are no more excuses for acting immature. No justification for making the same stupid mistakes. No more exemptions.

You no longer hear phrases like, "Well, she's young, or she'll grow out of that phase," or " she is so mature for her age."

I overheard a classroom teacher tell a five year old, "Act your age." I couldn't help but chuckle to myself. That kid was acting his age. He is five! What she really meant was, "Act older than you really are."

Being the youngest child in my family, I always thought of myself as the baby. I would argue that I never got away with much, but some would beg to differ.

Hitting a milestone is tough.

Hitting a deer is tougher.

I've hit two.

Now we don't live in a forest, and I don't drive through wild life preserves, but they come out of nowhere. Last month I hit a deer when I was going sixty miles per hour. I saw a flash of brown and white. That's it.

The airbag deployed; that's a nice way of saying: exploded. Smoke came out from under the dash and my face, hair and clothes were covered with slivers of black plastic from the steering wheel.

Now if someone actually devised this as a means of safety, I'd like to have that job. I could not see anything. Mind you, I was still traveling at sixty miles per hour. I eventually let off the gas and pulled over to the side of the highway.

As I started pushing the airbag back in to the sardine size compartment it came out of, I read the instructions:

Do not continue driving after the airbag has deployed.

I admit it was a little difficult to steer with all that stuff flapping around when I took a corner.

However, I called my mechanic who of course had fixed my vehicle from my first deer collision. He was calm and could tell I was not. He asked if the vehicle was drivable and reminded me to push in the airbag as much as possible. He also told me not to rub my eyes, since that powder-like chemical that causes the airbag to deploy could burn. (Who got paid for this invention?)

I finally arrived at the body shop and the owner proclaimed, "I asked God to increase His favor toward me today, and He has done that through you."

Now that was a voice filled with faith, but I really didn't want to hear it at the time. Unfortunately, that's when we probably need His word the most.

"For I am convinced that neither death nor life, neither angels nor demons, neither the present nor the future, nor any powers, neither height nor depth, nor anything else in all creation, will be able to separate us from the love of God that is in Christ Jesus our Lord."
Romans 8:38-39

Look What God Can Do

Hallelujah, Hallelujah
Glory Hallelujah look what God is doing through you
Angels are singing when the saints are bringing
Praise and adoration from each and every nation
Glory Hallelu, look what God can do

Jordan, Israel and France, Russia and Afghanistan
Zimbabwe and Cameroon
Children in Rumania, souls in Ethiopia
Longing to hear the news

How can they hear unless they're told
We must share the hope that we know
It's up to you to tell them what God can do
Satan trembles when he sees the weakest saint
Down on his knees
Heaven knows the power of prayer
Comfort when I feel afraid
A light when I've lost my way
Lifting burdens that I bear
You're always on my heart and mind
I know you pray for me and
I hope you know
You've shown me what God can do

People living in the street longing for some food to eat
Starving for somebody to care
When a child cries in the night
Is someone there to show the light
Let them know God is there
How can they see unless they're shown
Can they share the hope that we know
It's up to you to tell them what God can do

(Recorded on Revival's *Stone By Stone* c.d.)

Chapter Fifteen: Cold in the Valley

My husband and I had the privilege of living in Tennessee for awhile not long after we first got married. I have to admit that my favorite memory was riding with him on his motorcycle through the beautiful winding roads on the way to some friends' house for a devotional and campfire.

The ride there was exhilarating. The wind in my face, the smell of the pine trees, and the joy of being together.

The ride home was another story. The temperature had dropped when the sun had set, and every time we rode through a valley we were freezing. It became an endurance test. I started trying to remember how many valleys and hills we had remaining until we would make it to the warmth of our home.

The ride that had been so breathtaking was now literally "breath taking."

I've been on the top of a few mountains, and I've also seen my share of valleys. I've found that the longer I am in the valley, the more I need God's word, my family, spiritual music, and Christian friends to help get me out.

If I stay in the valley too long, it becomes a rut. You just keep going back and forth in the same tracks, hoping for different results but doing the same thing.

I was a counselor at a Christian camp one summer. It was hot and tiring but very rewarding. The young ladies in my group were amazing. One night we had our group devotional, and I asked the girls if they could spend time with anyone, living or already gone, who would it be.

There were some interesting answers: the pop singers of the day, a few apostles, and a few surprises. One young lady said, she would love to spend a day with her grandpa. I knew her grandparents, in fact her grandmother was the first Sunday School teacher I remember. She had given me a small, white leather *Bible* that belonged to her mother, and she always made me feel special.

I knew the girl's grandfather was still living and asked her why she chose him since they lived in the same city, and she could spend time with him whenever she wanted. She replied, "He won't always be there for me."

Last night, in our local paper, I read his obituary. My parents went to the service and the church was completely filled. Mom said that the most amazing thing about the funeral was that there were people from every walk of life; rich, poor, black, white, children and elderly. I thought back to his granddaughter's choice so many years ago. She was wise beyond her years.

In the same group at camp that evening was a young girl crying on her bunk bed. I walked over to her, and she handed me a letter she had received in the camp mail that day. It was filled with words of hatred and anger. Heartbreaking words from someone saying how grateful they were that she was not at home. Paragraphs stating how she could never compare to her sister.

I was shocked. I demanded to know who sent this letter to her. I was going to get to the bottom of this. She looked up and said, "My mom sent it."

Now, I have never felt at a loss of words like I did that evening. I could not comprehend a relationship with a mother that involved inflicting this much pain in your own child.

We remained silent for a while.

We finally prayed together, and I reassured her that she had a father in Heaven who longed to have her home. His letters would never crush her spirit.

That night as I lay in my bunk bed thinking about her letter, I read from the Book of John. John 15:15, "I no longer call you servants, because a servant does not know his master's business. Instead, I have called you friends."

I Call You Friend

I call you friend
The time we spend together goes so fast
Until the end In Heaven we know the time will last
God brings together two people of a kind
Through stormy weather a knot is tied that binds
The hearts of friends who need a listening ear
A shoulder to share a fallen tear
I call you friend
A friend is chosen, coincidence it seems
But hearts keep closer, the memories they bring
Though miles may separate us, we're never far apart
We share a special feeling in our hearts
I call you friend
When I feel helpless and no one can be found
His words remind me He'll never let me down
He picks me up when life just isn't fair
When hope is gone I know He hears my prayer
He calls me friend
I call you friend
Forever in my heart you will remain
Until the end
In Heaven I know we'll meet again

(Recorded on Revival's *Whatcha Gonna Do About It* c.d.)

"My intercessor is my friend as my eyes pour out tears to God; on behalf of a man he pleads with God as a man pleads for his friend." Job 16:20-21.

Chapter Sixteen: Finding Your Ministry

My parents worship at a church that has a cookie ministry. The first time I heard that, I must admit I chuckled. (I think my actual response was, "That sounds like my kind of ministry.") Mom explained that when a visitor comes and fills out an attendance card, they are met later that week at their front door by some friendly Christians with a dozen cookies and a simple "thank you for worshipping with us."

How great is that? I love it. Of course a ministry doesn't have to be cookies, and it doesn't have to be for a visitor. It can be your neighbor, it can be as simple as checking your local school to see if all the kids have crayons, or making sure everyone at the local nursing home receives a card on his or her birthday.

As an art teacher in our local school system, I've made it my goal every year to have my students make birthday cards for a neighboring rest home. The kids love it and the recipient smiles and the cards decorate the doors and rooms of the nursing home for weeks. It's especially fun when we pick an odd numbered year. Not 90 years old or some special number, but 83.

My favorite will always be Jenny Hazel Valentine. Her name was Hazel Sewell, but her birthday was on Valentine's Day. She was my neighbor for many years. I checked on her often and would take her little treats. When she broke her hip and had to be put in the nursing home, I missed her smiling face and sweet voice when she would see me pull up in front of our home, "Howdy, neighbor."

She called my husband Chet over one evening thinking her television was broken. She loved to watch baseball on television, so Chet went over and noticed the television was simply unplugged. She thought he was so handy when, within seconds, her beloved game was back on.

I knew on Valentine's Day, she would be celebrating her ninety-ninth birthday. I thought to myself, when you get to be 99, why wait to have a big party?

So my students made ninety-nine cards, and I took one of my classes over to the rest home and called the newspaper and brought balloons and cake and we had a great party! She was surrounded by children, and they were all smiles.

She quoted the poem I'd heard her recite many times:

Jenny Hazel Valentine
Curls her locks just like mine
Two in front & four behind
Jenny Hazel Valentine

Then she asked the students if any of them had a special name or tradition that went with their name. A little dark haired girl, raised her hand and smiled and said, "My name is Angel, and I was born on Christmas Day."

"That *is* special," Hazel replied.

She passed away not long after our special day with her. Her daughter sent me a beautiful card, and I cried and later she called me up and asked why I had chosen to make that day so special. I just replied, "Why not?"

Maybe cards are already your ministry. Perhaps you make it your goal to check on a set group of friends or widows each day and make sure they are doing okay.

Whether it is walking with a friend, helping in a neighbor's garden, or simply lifting someone up in prayer, find your ministry.

The Apostle Paul writes in Romans 12:6-8: "We have different gifts, according to the grace given us. If it is serving, let him serve, if it is teaching, let him teach, if it is encouraging, let him encourage, if it is contributing to the needs of others, let him give generously."

I challenge you right now to try to do something for someone else everyday. You'll start looking for something or someone to bless, and it will become a positive addiction.

A dear friend of mine, who has seen me through many struggles, said something that became a word of encouragement and then turned into a song. In the middle of a school hallway, realizing how discouraged I was, he said, "Had you been the only one, Christ would have still gone to Calvary." Within a few minutes, the Lord put this song on my heart.

Angels Sing Holy

Had you been the only one
He would've gone to Calvary
Angels are praying when you're on bended knee
When just one soul truly gives their heart to Him
Angels are singing, shouting
And bringing praises to the Lamb

Angels sing holy, holy, holy
Is the Lord God Almighty
Who was and is and is to come
And we sing holy, holy, holy
Is the Lord God Almighty
Who was and is and is to come

If He hadn't known the pain
If Christ hadn't felt that agony
Then we'd all been lost condemned eternally
When a child is born into the Father's family
I know Heaven rejoices, a chorus of voices
Singing glory to the King

Angels rejoice when a lost child's voice
Is heard singing the praise of the Lamb

And we sing holy, holy, holy
Is the Lord God Almighty
Who was and is and is to come
And we sing holy, holy, holy
Is the Lord God Almighty
Who was and is and is to come

And we sing holy, holy, holy
Is the Lord God Almighty
Who was and is and is to come

And we sing holy, holy, holy
Is the Lord God Almighty
Who was and is and is to come

(Recorded on Revival's *Knockin' At Your Door* c.d.)

"Each of the four living creatures had six wings and was covered with eyes all around, even under his wings. Day and night they never stop saying: "Holy, holy, holy is the Lord God Almighty, who was, and is, and is to come." Revelation 4:8.

Chapter Seventeen: Song Heard 'Round the World

There are times and situations when you look back and realize you were acting ugly. That's what a friend of mine calls it: 'Acting Ugly.'

Well, as I look back to a camp where we were preparing to sing next to the Black Sea in Ukraine, I realize *I* was 'Acting Ugly.'

We took a long, hot, crowded bus ride, and the driver got lost. He was cursing in Russian and our interpreter, Julia, was shaking her head in disgust.

The camp was empty, the gates were locked, and we were exhausted. I had not slept in three days. My sleep schedule could not adjust to the planes, trains and death-defying taxi rides, and now we had ridden on a bus to the middle of nowhere.

Our bass singer, Terry, an amazing eye doctor who had given free eye exams and glasses to hundreds of needy miners and elderly people and children in orphanages, was enjoying the breathtaking coast of the Black Sea, and headed down for a walk on the beach. It drove me crazy how he could find something good in everything. That's just not natural.

All I could think of was finding somewhere to prop my head up and cool off and maybe catch a nap. The four of us ended up sitting in a room, sweaty and thirsty, sharing the very last of the thirty, twelve ounce, water bottles from Sam's Wholesale, Donja, our alto, had carried for over 8000 miles.

I was frustrated and, in an angry outburst asked, "What are we even doing here?"

Each one looked at me shocked as the words came out of my mouth. Donja started to cry, Terry looked at the sea, and Craig, our tenor, looked at me with tears in his eyes and said,

"*You* are the reason we are here. Had you not started this group, written these songs, and kept at this for over fifteen years, we would not have come. There is no one on Earth, besides my family, that I would rather be with, and there are people here who have never heard the name of Jesus. *That's* why we are here."

"Love never gives up, never loses faith, is always hopeful, and endures through every circumstance." 1 Corinthians 13:7.

Immediately, this came pouring out of my mouth and my heart through tears:

Song Heard 'Round the World

There is a song heard 'round the world
It is for every boy and girl
It is a song of grace and love
We sing to you of Jesus blood
It starts within the human heart
A still small voice cut's through the dark
The tone and melody ring clear
And if you listen you can hear
There is a song heard 'round the world
It is for every boy and girl
It is a song of grace and love
We sing to you of Jesus blood
It finds a voice and hits the air
The message louder than a prayer
The chorus swells the verse resounds
God's love from Heaven has come down
There is a song heard 'round the world
It is for every boy and girl
It is a song of grace and love
We sing to you of Jesus blood

(Recorded on Revival's *Song Heard 'Round The World* c.d.)

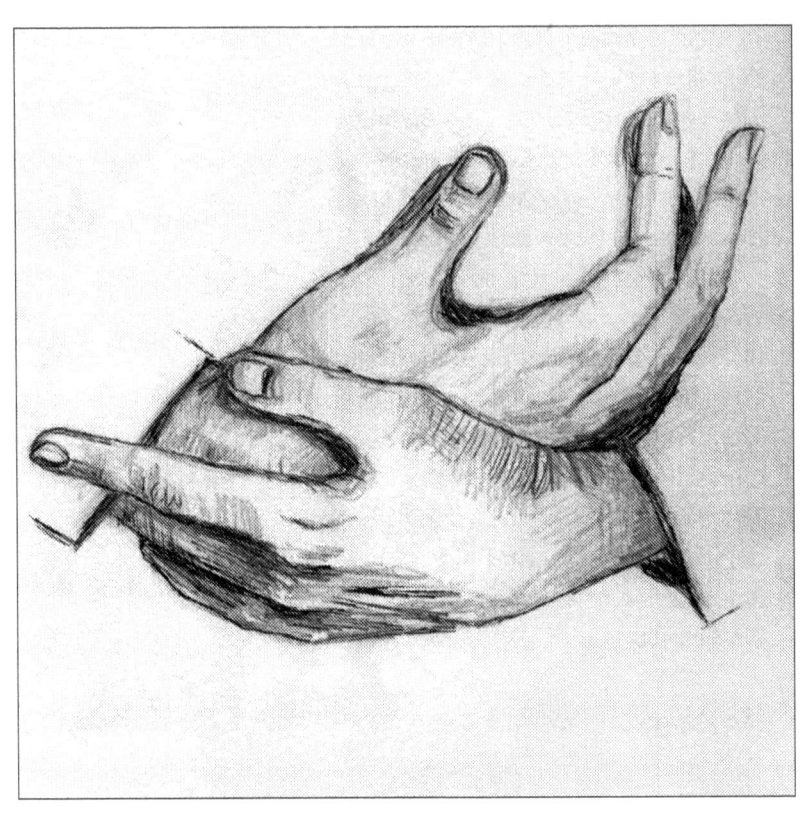

Chapter Eighteen: The Healing Power Of Prayer

There was a wonderful article, in a *Reader's Digest* I read recently, on the power of prayer. It stated that a study conducted in 2001 of women with a form of breast cancer, found that women who rated spirituality as important had a greater number of circulating white blood cells and stronger immune systems than those who did not (Bain, 2005). Now I'm not a huge fan of statistics and even less a fan of medical studies, but this one made me smile.

Dr. Koenig found that those who prayed daily and attended religious services weekly had 40% less hypertension than those who didn't pray or go to services. A 2004 study linked church attendance with living longer.

I'm convinced of the power of prayer, and God's will in my life, and to know that someone is out there measuring it with cells and systems simply brings me joy.

You can't measure the healing power of prayer, but you can count on it. You can't explain faith to someone who doesn't believe, but you can trust your life and soul with it.

We were preparing to sing in York, Nebraska, and the college there put us up in the dorms for the evening. My husband and I were talking about how good God has been to us, and we started writing this song together. He's an audio sound man so the last verse using the word, "amplify" was definitely his. It's become one of my favorite phrases.

My Prayer

Was it so very long ago
You came to live on Earth
When will I ever comprehend the power of the Savior's birth.
A man with rough but gentle hands
A carpenter by trade
I want so much to understand
The sacrifice the Father gave.
And in the silence I can hear a voice that calls to me
Sometimes it comes in loud and clear
Sometimes I'm just not listening.
The rain has come
The wind has blown
And stronger for the storm I stand
Amazing Grace I've come to know
While clinging tightly to His hand
Lord help me hear that voice inside
The message coming through
Please take my heart and amplify
The love I have for You

(Recorded on Revival's *Don't Wait 'til Winter* c.d.)

Chapter Nineteen: Consider It Pure Joy

We just had a family get together.

As we gathered in a circle holding hands, ready to pray for the food, there stood my two uncles, three aunts, several cousins, nieces and nephews and my parents. As my dad was praying for the food, my cousin's four-year old daughter set her sites on the one thing on the table she could not resist. There was a warm box of fried chicken, tender bar-b-cue brisket, corn on the cob and an American flag cake made of strawberries for the red stripes and blueberries for the field of stars. But this kid made a bee-line for a handful of Tootsie Pops. As we finished the prayer we all raised our heads, and there she stood grinning from ear to ear with a hand full of candy. Nothing looked better on that beautiful table than that store bought candy.

To her, it was pure sugar.
Pure fun.
Pure joy.

Kids understand pure joy. Can you remember being so excited you could hardly breathe? No, not that "out-of-breath-because-I-just-climbed-a-flight-of-stairs-feeling." I'm talking about that "Christmas morning-feeling" when it is all you can do not to scream or wiggle or shout.

I must admit, it has been a while since I've known that kind of joy. I remember when cassette tape recorders first came out. I know that ages me. As an eager ten-year old, I knew if I could have a cassette recorder for Christmas, I would be happy forever! I could tape myself on the guitar, I could record my sister when she was being mean (which no one ever believed), and I could record my favorite songs from the radio for free.

Mom kept asking what I wanted for Christmas, and I would give her no other answer: "A portable cassette recorder and batteries might be nice." Christmas finally arrived, and I opened my gift and let out a squeal. Happiness had been achieved. Where would I start recording first? I had so many ideas. Would you believe it even came with a little microphone? I could hardly sit still waiting for the little package that I knew had the batteries. I decided my first recording would be capturing Mom and Dad talking about what great kids we were and how much we appreciated our gifts.

The only mistake I made, well, one of the many mistakes I made, was doing it secretly, in their bedroom, when they thought I was asleep in my room. Little did I know that when the sixty-minute tape runs out, there's a large audible click when it shuts off. I also didn't know that parents talk about other things besides their children. Needless to say, I was grounded for far too long, and lost the use of my cassette recorder for the first month of the year. My pure joy disappeared very quickly, but it was a lesson well learned.

From that time forward, I had restrictions of what I could record, who I could record, and when I could record. My joy was limited, my plans were grounded, and my punishment was effective. It was difficult to consider that pure joy.

However, James 1:2 states, "consider it pure joy when you face trials of many kinds because the testing of your faith develops perseverance." Sometimes it takes a while to realize that our heart's desire, may not bring us happiness.

Have you ever thought through the way something was supposed to be and then realized you have absolutely no control over it? The only thing we can control is our attitude and how we deal with situations. I remember being a stubborn redhead about the age of ten when my father said, "That attitude is going to get you into trouble young lady."

Most of the time it did (or does).

I have found that same attitude has affected my relationship with friends, family and co-workers. I even did research in college trying to understand my attitude. Being a fair-skinned redhead, I learned that due to the light pigmentation of my skin, my reaction time to difficult situations was often much shorter than the reaction time of others.

Not that this information should be used as an excuse, but my beautician even told me, after having four redheads in her family, that she knew redheads were much more tender headed. As a teenager, I just thought it was hormonal when I would blow up or argue with someone over nothing. I've really tried to be aware of my competitive nature and proclivity toward losing my temper. I'm not saying it is easy, but with concentration it can be done.

James continues, "Perseverance must finish its work so that you may be mature and complete, not lacking in anything." (James 1: 4). I love that 'not lacking in anything' part. It's the perseverance that's tough.

There is not much in life that annoys me as much as mosquitoes. I hate mosquitoes. If there are twenty people standing outside, I will be the one in twenty to get bit. I have this theory, that since I have diabetes, my blood sugar is sometimes high; therefore, my blood is sweeter, and the mosquitoes know it.

Okay, so it sounds ridiculous, but I currently have six mosquito bites on my legs, and it is *only* the third day of summer. They definitely persevere when it comes to finding me.

I don't spend that much time outside, but they find me. I was thinking of the scripture, 'consider it pure joy,' and I realized how tough that truly is. What are mosquitoes good for? Do they not carry disease and cause skin irritation? Neither of those reasons makes sense. I just don't know. I can't think of one good reason they exist.

But God in his infinite wisdom has set nature and everything in its place.

Where am I going with all this? Glad you asked.

You know how there are the big things we pray to God about, like cancer, loved ones, traveling mercies, job concerns. Then there are the little things at the bottom of the list, like a shorter check out line at the grocery store, or a letter or call from a friend you've been thinking about.

Perhaps you, like me, start to get a little sleepy toward the end of your evening prayer, and we don't even take that little pesky worry that has been flying around us like a mosquito to the Father and God of All Mankind because we're afraid it is too small for Him.

I love the way Matthew 6:26 reveals, "Look at the birds of the air; they do not sow or reap or store away in barns, and yet your heavenly Father feeds them. Are you not much more valuable than they?" Does God not care about what happens in your life, no matter how small it seems to the rest of the world? He knows every concern, every problem, every pain."

I was traveling with a friend the other day, and I noticed a mosquito in the car. I screamed, "Mosquito, KILL IT!" Thirty seconds later, "SPLAT!!!" right against the passenger window. This insect had already had one of us for lunch. I was so excited when my friend killed that bug, it was almost embarrassing. I just didn't want to think about a hovering insect leaving an itching welt on my freckled ankles for the next two hours of our trip.

As I reflected at the end of the day, I began to write in my journal three things I'm grateful for: a safe trip, a good friend, a car with air conditioning, and I must admit, I was tempted to include the death of that mosquito. It was minor, I know, but I was still grateful.

I was reading in the Book of Titus, in the New Testament and found this scripture: "He saved us, not because of righteous things we had done, but because of His mercy. He saved us through the washing of rebirth and renewal by the Holy Spirit." Titus 3:5.

It was a wonderful reminder that I will never be good enough or strong enough. I will never be perfect. God knew that. In fact he planned on it. That's why His mercy, which is made new every morning, covers me. Thank God, He saved us.

He Saved Us

He saved us
Not because of righteous things we've done
He saved us
Through the washing of His precious blood
He saved us through the sacrifice of His only Son
Through His mercy we're saved by Love

It is with a grateful heart that I come to you today
It is with humble adoration
That I take this time to say
I know that I'm not all I could be
And I don't always see
That He's beside me and to guide me and to comfort me

If you've got a troubled mind
And you can find no rest
If you've been worried 'bout the future
And you wonder if you're blessed
I know that He's got all that I need
And He can always see
When I am falling I can call and He will rescue me

(Recorded on Revival's *Knockin' At Your Door* c.d.)

"He is the God who avenges me, who puts the nations under me, who sets me free from my enemies. You exalted me above my foes; from violent men You rescued me. Therefore I will praise You, O Lord, among the nations; I will sing praises to Your name." 2 Samuel 22:48-50.

Chapter Twenty: Don't Wait 'Til Winter

I grew up going to Flint Hills Christian Camp. Some of my favorite memories are the evening hikes we took, winning a Bible for memorizing the most Bible verses, and singing, 'Round the flagpole, you must go', for putting our elbows on the table in the chow hall.

Our music group had the privilege of going back to the camp several times to sing. There is one camp session I will never forget.

A group of young people had come up to participate in the camp from Winnsboro, Texas. On their way home, they were listening to a song we had sung entitled, "Don't Wait 'til Winter". A young man named Kyle told his friend he needed to become a Christian. He knew what he needed to do and had put it off.

His friend told him that just because camp was over, it was still not too late. So as they made the drive home, they talked with their preacher, they stopped at the church building, and Kyle was baptized.

I received a letter from his friend six months later.

Kyle was involved in an accident and was killed. The youth group was shaken, and they couldn't help but think about Kyle's decision to become a Christian.

The next summer at camp, we were asked to come back and sing. As we arrived, I noticed Kyle's picture on the mantel on the fireplace behind us.

I didn't know if I could make it through the song, but knew I had to try. Tears filled the eyes of the young people, and they put their arms around each other and hearts were opened.

That evening, in the camp swimming pool over a dozen teenagers were baptized into Christ. I thank God for Kyle and his commitment. I thank God for using us in spite of ourselves. I thank God for the hearts of the young.

"Unless you become like a little child you can not enter the kingdom of Heaven." (Matthew 18: 2-3)

Don't Wait 'til Winter

If you need to right a wrong, don't wait 'til winter
If you need to atone, don't wait 'til winter
The winds of winter blow so cold, no one will have time for you
    when you're sick and old
If you want Christ to save your precious soul, don't wait 'til
    winter
If you need to make a change, don't wait 'til winter
If you die in your sins, Lord what a shame, don't wait 'til winter
The winds of winter make the warmest heart turn cold
You might not even feel it should, the winds begin to blow
And if a sister has left the fold, don't wait 'til winter
You must go and try to gently bring her home, oh don't wait 'til
    winter
Now if you need, need to come to Christ, don't wait 'til winter
You need to be baptized, don't wait 'til winter
I'm praying you come before winter
You know you've got to come before winter
I beg you to come before winter

(Recorded on Revival"s *Don't Wait 'Til Winter* c.d.)

"I will hasten and not delay to obey your commands." Psalm 119:60.

Chapter Twenty-One: My Bible and Its Scars

On the way back from a singing trip to Texas, we smelled something burning. When Chet looked in his rearview mirror, he saw smoke coming from the back of our van.

We pulled off I-35 and onto an exit ramp in Oklahoma City around 11:00 p.m. By the time we pulled over into an empty lot beside a Denny's restaurant, there were flames engulfing the back of our vehicle. I reached in the side door to grab my leather purse which contained my billfold and insulin, and Chet hollered to leave it, the van was going to blow up.

He grabbed my purse, and I ran to the Denny's to call 911.

I'm sure I've been hysterical before, but I don't remember it ever being as vivid as that evening. The manager reassured me they saw the flames and had already called the fire department which was only minutes away.

Within five minutes time, the flames hit one of the gas tanks, which was almost completely filled, and then it exploded. The windows of the van burst, and we could see the interior melting.

I kept thinking about clothes and things that were in the back. I just started sobbing. Chet was already thinking ahead. He's so good in a crisis. That's one of his gifts. I freak. He functions. His concern went immediately to our trailer, which contained all of our sound equipment, and was attached to the back of the burning van.

The fire trucks arrived and started dousing the van with water. Seconds later, the second gas tank exploded. Chet begged them to try and save the trailer and equipment, and they did.

As we sat, watching our vehicle smolder in the cool Oklahoma night air, a small, older woman came up to us. Her clothes were tattered, and she appeared out of nowhere.

She looked at me, and looked at the van, and said,

"You all right, ma'am?"

"Our van caught fire, and we live in Kansas, and what are we going to do?"

She asked calmly, "Were you doing the Lord's work?"

I said, "Yes, I believe we were."

She said, "That's why you are out here and not in there." Chet and I looked at each other wondering who she was and where she had come from, and when we turned back to her, she was gone.

This next poem has not been turned into a song. Not yet, anyway.

My Bible and Its Scars

It didn't burn for very long
Those treasures that were ours
The clothes, the tapes and our c.d.'s
My Bible with its scars

The smoke that caused my eyes to cry
And destroyed Earthly things
Could not destroy our faith in God
Or keep my soul from singing

For though we love what we've been given
It's nothing when compared
To those we love and Him above
Who keeps us in His care.

Afterword

I was inspired to start writing after an event occurred almost twenty years ago.

While traveling across the country with a Christian Music group called Acappella, our red Silver Eagle bus pulled into our all too familiar lunch stop, McDonald's.

Perhaps it was the fact that I could not stomach another Chicken McNugget, or because I was coming down with the flu, but either way, I decided to stay on the bus while the other singers and bus driver, who happened to be my husband, went on in.

Not fifteen minutes passed until I became too sick to remain on the bus. As I stepped off, I located the first restroom I could find. When I returned twenty minutes later, the parking lot was empty. The bus was gone.

What I thought was a poor joke, soon became a predicament. I began to consider my options. Wait for the bus to return, flag down a semi truck and have him radio ahead to the bus, or begin walking in the direction I knew we were headed.

It soon became evident that they must not know I was not on board the bus. We always did a head count to make sure everyone was accounted for, but I had put a blanket over my bunk to keep the light out. I tightened my shoe laces and zipped my coat and headed toward Corsicana, Texas.

Every highway horror story I had heard or seen began to flash through my mind. I knew at least my husband would eventually realize I was not on the bus and come to find me. I just kept walking and waiting for that big red bus to come over the hill and pick me up. I was on the highway with no phone number, no name of where we were singing and no idea where I was going.

Now, I'm no expert, but it seemed to me that being the only female on a bus with five men for months at a time, you might notice when a freckle-faced redheaded female was missing. I was sorely mistaken.

After thirty minutes of walking, I was tired, cold, mad and hurt. Hopelessly stranded, before the age of cell phones, I began to envision spending the rest of the month working as a drive-thru clerk at McDonald's to earn enough for bus fare home. I decided I had two new choices:

Pray.
Call the Highway Patrol.

I did both.

About that time, I located a phone at a nearby business, and explained my situation to the secretary. After she finished laughing, she gave me the phone.

Within minutes, the local sheriff was taking me to the county line, at which point the neighboring sheriff picked me up and took me to the next county line. During my transfers from car to car, the Highway Patrol had located the bus and pulled them over.

My husband had driven 100 miles and still had not realized he was missing a special passenger. When he was finally pulled over and asked if he was missing someone, his mouth dropped open as he realized I was not on board.

The road manager assessed the situation and decided they did not have time to come and get me and make it to the concert in time. Co-incidentally, a group of convicts was being transferred to a new location by their sheriff, and they had room for one more. Me.

The conversation varied from country music, to armed robbery, and then I shared my story which they all found hilarious. Three sheriffs, and two squad cars, and one van loaded with inmates who were separated from the driver by a metal fence, and three hours later, and I arrived at our concert location to find my husband crawling on his knees toward the loading dock, with his hands folded in prayer asking for forgiveness for leaving me behind.

In that split second, my anger, my frustration, my fear was gone. I was filled with thankfulness that they had not left me on purpose, and that I was back where I belonged.

No blinding light hit me on the road to Corsicana, but I am convinced that road served it's purpose that chilly winter's day. I was given an opportunity to look at my life, my attitude and my purpose.

I began writing songs after that.

I became open to new possibilities.

Most of us know when we stumble. It's the getting back up each time that's tough.

I hope this book helps you to get back up one more time.

Bibliography

Bain, Julie. "The Healing Power of Prayer," *Readers Digest*, April 2005, p. 153.

Beresford, Bruce, director. *Tender Mercies*, DVD, Antron Media Production, 1983.

Crosby, Fanny & Mrs. E.L. Knapp. *Blessed Assurance*, 1873.

Fogelberg, Dan. "Along the Road," *Phoenix*. Full Moon/ Epic Records, 1980.

Frost, Evelyn. *3,000 Quotations on Christian Themes*. Carroll E. Simcox, editor. Baker Book House, #2110, p. 178.

Lucado, Max. *It's Not About Me: Rescue From the Life We Thought Would Make Us Happy*. Thomas Nelson, 2004.

Shapiro, Tom. "If There Hadn't Been You," *The Very Best of Billy Dean*. Capitol Records, 2005.

Hsu, Albert Y. *Singles @ the Crossroads*. InterVarsity Press, 1997.

Whately, Richard. *3,000 Quotations on Christian Themes*. Carroll E. Simcox, editor. Baker Book House, #2135, p. 179.

"Weekending," *Women's Devotional Bible*, New International Version. Zondervan Publishing, 1995, .p. 1044.

Extensive effort was made by both author and publisher to determine authorship of the song on page 28. If anyone knows this information, please forward it to the publisher for inclusion in future printings of this book.

Revival

Back row from left to right: Craig Hayes, Chet Sweet, Dr. Terry Lewis
Front row from left to right: Donja Cary, Danice Sweet

Revival Discography

Spirituals: I'll Fly Away, Deep River, Don't Wait 'til Winter, Wonderful, Precious Lord Take My Hand, Move Satan, He Never Lied To Me, Roll Jordan Roll, Dig A Little Deeper, God is Good, All the Time, I Love To Praise Him, Were You There, Hold To God's Unchanging Hand, Give Me Jesus.

Song Heard Round the World: Were You There, Give Me Jesus, I Just Want to Be Where You Are, Because of Him, His Love, I Love To Praise Him, I Must Share Jesus, I Wanna Know More, God Is So Good, When God Dips His Love In My Heart, Alleluia.

If That Isn't Love (voted in the top ten a cappella c.d.'s of all time): Old Country Church, Jesus He Will Fix It, Blessed Be The Name, He Calls Me His Child, Dig A Little Deeper, I Want To Be Just Like You, God is Good, We Are Gathered, Joyful Noise, Weep O Mine Eyes, Homecoming Day.

Best of Revival: Hurry Home, Amazing Grace, Angels Sing Holy, My Prayer, Deep River, Praying For You, Tender Mercies, If There Were No You, Restore My Soul, Whale Motel, Worship With Your Life, Satan's Been Riding Me Hard Blues, Humbly, No Run Of The Mill Messiah, Stone By Stone, Look What God Can Do.

Show Me The Cross: The Lord Bless & Keep You, I'm Just A Stranger Here, Someday, I Don't Mind, Climbin' Up the Mountain, There Must Be A City, If There Were No You, In Heaven There Won't Be No Blues, Zephaniah 3:17, Peanut Butter Song.

Under Construction (with the children's group Revelation): Exalt The Lord, Listen & Obey, New Wine, John Started Dreaming, Fruit Of The Spirit, God Made Everything, My Rock, My Shield, Whale Motel, Worship With Your Life.

Never Grow Old: Wayfaring Stranger, Precious Lord Take My Hand, O Sacred Head Are You Washed, Feeling Mighty Fine, This Is The Day, Enter His Gates, Working On A Building, Restore My Soul, My Lord Arose, Hold To God's Unchanging Hand.

Stone By Stone: Look What God Can Do, Sweet, Sweet Spirit, Spiritual Life, Life Eternal, He Never Lied To Me, I've Got A Father, Roll Jordan Roll, Floating Zoo, Mercy Lord.

Knockin' At Your Door: Praising Jesus, Home Where I Belong, Upper Room, Praying For You, Angels Sing Holy, He Saved Us, Sweet Hour Of Prayer, At The Name Of Jesus, Tender Mercies.

Whatcha Gonna Do About It: Beulah Land, Humbly, Send A Revival, I Will Speak Your Name, Never Say Goodbye, Everybody Will Be Happy Over There, I Call You Friend, Create A Change In Me, Satan's Been Ridin' Me Hard Blues, Idle Words, Nothing Like The Feeling of Harmony.

Don't Wait 'Til Winter: He's Lord of All, Unclouded Day, Whale Motel, On Zion's Glorious Summit, It Was His Will, I Want To Praise Him, Wonderful, No Run Of The Mill Messiah, You've Got To Go, Move Satan.

Walk In Jerusalem: Do You Believe, The Gentle Healer, Do What You Gotta Do, Soon I'm Going Home, I'll Fly Away, Deep River, You Don't Knock, Infants Tossed To & Fro, Let The Words, Psalms 137:1.

Revival's website is located at http://members.aol.com/revivalol/revival.htm or email Danice Sweet at dsweet@onemain.com.

PEARSON PUBLISHING COMPANY
CORPUS CHRISTI, TEXAS

For a complete list and description of our publications and to order books please go to our website:

www.PearsonPub.US

Catching the Dream: A Parent's Guide to Children's Dreams
    By Janet S. Gould $26.95

Consider It Joy. Includes CD.
    By Danice E. Sweet $16.95

Deal Me In
    By Alyce Guynn with illustrations by Jesse Taylor
    $23.95

His Angels Are In Charge
    By Frances Cotten Woodard $24.95

Floating Zoo and the Whale Motel. Includes CD.
    By Danice Sweet $26.95

Slumbertime: A Parent's Guide for Children's Sleep and Sleep Disorders
    By Janet S. Gould

For pricing and information on our other publications go to our website.

To mail in orders, send (1) a list of titles with number of copies of each title, (2) check or money order for total retail price of all books, plus (3) $5.00 shipping and handling for each book, and (4) your name and mailing address printed clearly, to:

Pearson Publishing Company
711 N. Carancahua, Suite 119
Corpus Christi, Texas 78475

www.ingramcontent.com/pod-product-compliance
Lightning Source LLC
Chambersburg PA
CBHW072159100426
42738CB00011BA/2468